C000143357

The Spirit and Liturgy

Jeremy Fletcher

Priest-in-Charge of St Andrew, Skegby
with All Saints, Stanton Hill and St Katherine, Teversal

Christopher Cocksworth

Director of the Southern Theological Education
and Training Scheme (STETS)

GROVE BOOKS LIMITED
RIDLEY HALL RD CAMBRIDGE CB3 9HU

Contents

Acknowledgements

The origins of this booklet lie in an idea by Jeremy Fletcher to lead a joint seminar on the Spirit and Liturgy at New Wine 1997. We are grateful to David Pytches for encouragement to go ahead with the seminar and to the Group for the Renewal of Worship (GROW) for its enthusiasm to see the thrust of the seminar written up in Grove booklet form. We are also grateful to the Group for its advice (especially to James Steven and Charles Read), to Ian Paul for his patience, to Keith Hubbard for his analysis and knowledge, and to Annie Robertson for delivering Chris and Charlotte's fifth child and, in so doing, inspiring some charismatic-liturgical thinking.

The Cover Illustration is by Mel Durrant

Copyright © Jeremy Fletcher and Christopher Cocksworth 1998

First Impression April 1998
ISSN 0144-1728
ISBN 1 85174 370 7

1
Introduction

Recently we had a new baby born into the family. Experiences of birth connect one very deeply to the work of the Spirit. The Hebrews called the Spirit the *ruach YHWH*, the breath of the Lord. As the very vitality of God, the Spirit carries the word that brings creation into being (Gen 1.1–3), sustains all that exists in life (Psalm 104.29), reanimates that which appears dead (Ez 37.1–14) and will renew the face of the earth on the Day of the Lord. The early Christians called the Spirit *'the Spirit of life'* (Rom 8.2). They had experienced this reanimating power of end-time strength (Dan 12.2). The fourth century church (in the Nicene-Constantinople creed of 381) called the Spirit *'the Lord and giver of life.'* The drafters of the creed knew that the Spirit's intimate and intrinsic involvement in the work of creation and new creation required that the Spirit be placed on the divine side. They said boldly that the Spirit is not just the means by which God gives life but is God himself giving life.

The Spirit's life-giving work feels very close when a child is being born. The messianic imagery of the birth-pangs of the kingdom and the labour of the Spirit is readily to hand. The deep sighs of painful expectation (Rom 8.18–27), the rush of breaking waters (Ez 43.2; 47.1–12), the overwhelming joy when the child breaks into the new world and breathes its air (John 16.21) make you feel that you have tuned into the pulse of God. The unfolding drama of birth also leaves you convinced that you are moving with a rich tradition of inherited words, actions and sequences which, in the hands of a skilful midwife, allow the new life to arrive as intended.

I have seen five children born and observed five midwives in action. Although each birth has been unique and each midwife has had to adapt to its special features, I have been fascinated by the limited repertoire of each occasion. There has been an inevitable order to the births. They have begun with the contractions of the mother and ended with the sounds of the child's voice, with necessary stages in between. The stages have all been of different lengths and have been handled in different ways but they have always happened. Midwife, mother and father have all related differently to each other and to the circumstances and yet the words said which really counted were almost identical every time and, I suspect, very similar to most other births which have ever taken place.

I was especially aware of the interplay between life and liturgy during this recent birth. Annie, our midwife, is an expert at *working with* rather than *intervening in* the natural flow of the birth. She was certainly the most charismatic of our midwives, not just because she was praying in tongues during the latter stages of the birth (!), but also because she was prepared to sit lightly to some of the traditions. I think this made her the best liturgist of the five. She did not open the manual at the beginning and work through it to the end. She had learnt to know the ways of birth—the fundamental flow of birth or, in the language of liturgists, its deep *structures*. Within this structure and sensitive to the natural movement of this particular life-giving event, she applied the inherited words and actions of midwifery at the necessary (and predictable) points, making them her own and, at times, adding her own to them.

Liturgy is not a warped ecclesiastical device designed to suppress the God-given creativity of Spirit-inspired worship.[1] It is, or should be, a handmaid of the Lord. The very word *liturgy* is derived from an association of Greek words which have to do with corporate, public service. Any authentic service we perform as Christians is a Spirit-inspired response to the work of God. We would not be able to make it without the enabling of the Spirit. Worship is the preeminent example of our obedient response to God. Inspired by the Spirit we give ourselves in song and dance, word and silence, body and spirit to God in loving adoration for the praise of his glory. Liturgy, therefore, is simply the way we respond to the life-giving work of God in the activity of worship. More technically it refers to how we *structure* our response to God and to how we articulate our response through the use of *words* and *actions*, particularly the words and actions which are said and done in *common*.

---

1   For a robust and racy rationale of the interdependence between charismatic worship and good liturgy, together with a wealth of practical advice, see John Leech, *Living Liturgy: a Practical Guide to Using Liturgy in Spirit-led Worship* (Eastbourne: Kingsway, 1997).

2
Liturgy and the Work of the Spirit

Theological Foundations

We have said that every authentic response to God is enabled by the Spirit. This is borne out by a quick look at references to worship in the New Testament. Preaching takes place 'in power and in the Holy Spirit' (1 Thess 1.5). Baptism is 'in the one Spirit' (1 Cor 12.13). Christ is confessed as Lord 'by the Spirit of God' (1 Cor 12.3). Christians are sealed for their future redemption by 'the Holy Spirit' (Eph 4.30). Songs are sung to the Lord by those who are 'filled with the Spirit' (Eph 5.18–19).

Worship in the New Testament is therefore by definition *in the Spirit*. It is also *through* Christ and *to* the Father (Eph 2.18). Even in the earliest stages of the worshipping life of the first Christians this fundamental trinitarian structure can be detected.[2] It is this which provides Christian worship with its deepest structure. God has revealed himself as Father through Christ the Son by means of the Spirit. God has saved us by drawing us by the Spirit into the humanity redeemed by Christ, so that we may share in the Son's life of love with the Father. This pattern of revelation and salvation structures every aspect of Christian existence, including our worship:

> And because you are children, God has sent
> the Spirit of his Son into our hearts, crying
> 'Abba! Father!' (Gal 4.6).

In Paul's preservation of the Aramaic *Abba* we can see one of the earliest examples of the evolution of Christian liturgical texts. As well as the Spirit initiating us into the basic structure of Christian worship, the Spirit also gives us words to articulate our worship. *Abba* (Father) is one such word; Lord Jesus (1 Cor 12.3; Phil 2.11) are two others. The Spirit led the first—and Jewish—Christians to name God *Abba* and to confess Christ as *Kyrios* (Lord) in their worship. And, what is more, because the Spirit brought people into a common faith, the Spirit-inspired words of worship were necessarily common texts of the various first-century Christian communities and they became embodied in the written forms of prayer as they began to emerge.

The Spirit relates us to Christ as Lord, and through Christ to the Father of the Son, because the Spirit loves the Father and the Son and holds the Father and

---

2   For further evidence see Christopher J Cocksworth, *Holy, Holy, Holy: Worshipping the Trinitarian God* (London: DLT, 1997).

the Son together in an eternal embrace of love. Another wonder which has struck me afresh with the birth of a new child into the family is the way children are both an expression of their parent's love and a way by which they love each other. This is an inevitably inadequate but nonetheless useful picture of the Spirit. The Spirit can be seen as the expression of the Father's love for the Son and thus as the gift of the Father's love to the Son. Likewise the Spirit is the expression of the Son's responding love for the Father and so the gift of the Son's love to the Father.[3] The Spirit is, to use a traditional title, the *bond of communion* between the Father and the Son. However, the Spirit is not, as it were, swallowed up in the love between Father and Son any less than a child is simply a feature of her parents' love. Rather, the Spirit is released by the loving of Father and Son into a distinct personhood, so that he is, using a less traditional title, the *friend of love*. The Spirit, as the child or friend of love between Father and Son, is poured out from the rich and full life of God to be a friend of love beyond God, by birthing into being that which has no being (Rom 4.17), by binding it together into an interconnected whole and by bringing it into unity with God. The Spirit is therefore, to use a more familiar description, *the Spirit of fellowship* (2 Cor 13.13; Phil 2.1). In the Spirit the Son and the Father have fellowship with each other and speak words of love to each other. In the Spirit we have fellowship with the Son and the Father and we speak words of love to the Son and through the Son to the Father. In the Spirit we have fellowship with each other and speak words of love to each other.

The Language of Love

The language of love involves time-honoured words and actions and time-honoured ways of structuring those words and actions *together with* spontaneous words and actions. Just think of the words you use to express your love of another. Probably a number of these are time-honoured phrases which have been passed on to you through the culture, many of them very ancient in origin. Others may have evolved from your own loving relationship, perhaps also beginning in the formative stages of your loving. Most of these time-honoured phrases will once have been spontaneous words and actions that, over time, have become fixed and formal, though still feel fresh on the lips and are able to speak to the heart. The most structured and time-honoured way of speaking words of love between a man and a woman are the vows of the marriage service. The words of even the proposed Church of England, Roman Catholic and Methodist revisions have changed very little since the twelfth century, except that the bride no longer promises to be 'bonnie and buxom in bed'[4] and the

---

3   For further development of these ideas see Thomas A Smail, *The Giving Gift* (London: DLT, 1994) and Cocksworth, *Holy, Holy, Holy, op cit*, pp 179-182.
4   As in the Sarum Marriage rite; see F E Brightman, *The English Rite*, Vol 2 (London: Rivingtons, 1915) p 804.

general promise of bridal obedience is at most optional. In substance the marriage vows have been regarded as unsurpassable ways of voicing love by generations of people.

With Valentine's Day just around the corner at the time of writing, it is not difficult to find other examples of expressions of love through received and common words and actions. Yet, as any pair of lovers know, words and actions, however good in themselves, only become the right words and actions when used at the right time and in the right way. They need careful planning if they are to do their job properly, even if the careful planning is designed to create an environment in which they can be used at a spontaneous moment. They also need to be used authentically. They may be in a different register from one's everyday speech but they must resonate with what is said in less formal ways so that they can be owned by the speaker and hearer. Valentine Day's expressions of love have a public character to them. They can be seen and shared with others. They are likely to be more stylized than that which is said in more private moments between two people but again they need to be consistent with what is said and done when there is nobody to observe. The words themselves therefore derive their true meaning from the context of the whole relationship in which they are used. Isolated from this loving context they become noisy gongs and clashing cymbals.

Clearly the language of love is complex and multi-layered but it certainly embraces both the fixed and the free, the given and spontaneous, the received and the newly made. The Spirit who inspires all genuine gestures of love directs our worship through both time-tested texts and actions (as they are properly applied within the given structures to particular acts of worship) and spontaneous words and actions (as they are activated in the private depths of a person or shared by those so moved with the corporate body of worshippers).

This is how the activity of the Spirit can be discerned in the formative history of the worship to which we now turn.

The Origins of Our Worship

The Spirit gave to the people of Israel texts of worship. Inspired by the Spirit individuals crafted creeds, such as the Shema (Deut 6.4), hymns, such as the Songs of Moses and Hannah, and prayers, such as some of the psalms, Aaron's blessing, Nehemiah's thanksgiving and a variety of other material. These were refined through use and reflection and passed down through the generations as key liturgical resources for forming and expressing Israel's unique relationship with God. The synagogue worship Jesus would have experienced was a combination of received, common texts set within a predictable order, spontaneous prayers following certain conventions, and a flexibility ready to respond to opportunities of the moment (such as the invitation to Jesus, a visiting 'rabbi,' to read the lesson and expound its meaning in Nazareth's synagogue).

Although the overwhelming experience of the outpouring of the Spirit made early Christian worship radically different from the contemporary worship of the synagogue, the underlying mix of form and freedom continued. The charismatic character of New Testament worship is now generally accepted by biblical commentators, even if it is not always acknowledged by liturgical scholars. Early Christian worship was saturated with the sense that—as Gordon Fee, the Pentecostal scholar, puts it—*God's empowering presence* was in their midst.[5] The eschatological promise of salvation was being fulfilled. The conditions of the end-time were invading the space and time of the present. The tongues of angels had come to earth and the tongues of mortals were being understood (1 Cor 13.1; 14.5). The wisdom of God hidden in the depths of God was being made known (1 Cor 2.9–13). Healings were happening (Acts 3.1–10). Exultant joy was being felt (Acts 2.46). Kingdom love was being shared (Acts 2.44–5).

But running alongside this dynamically new experience of worship were three features which provided a framework and gave some fixed points to a potentially chaotic phenomenon. First, there was the sort of leadership which people like Paul exercised. With their roots in the ordered informality of the synagogue, Paul and others like him developed guidelines for the construction of new liturgical skins to hold the intoxicating new wine of Christian worship. Second, despite the differences between Christian and Jewish worship, respect for the liturgical inheritance ran strong. Jewish texts—psalms, prayer forms and doxologies—were taken up into Christian worship and were injected with new life by Christological connections. Third, Spirit-inspired texts were remembered, repeated and circulated amongst the Christian communities, becoming part of the common Christian worship material. Often these began in song. An interesting example can be found in Paul's credal summary in Romans 1.3–4 which, if we follow C K Barrett's translation, includes two lines of Hebrew style parallelism:

> in the sphere of the flesh, born of the family David;
> in the sphere of the Holy Spirit, appointed Son of God.[6]

It is quite likely that this was a pre-Pauline song which evolved in the Spirit-filled worship of an early Christian community and passed into the hands of other communities to be used for both worship and teaching.

Evidence from the second century indicates that Christian worship became more sure of its basic framework, somewhat more precise about its fixed texts but also ready to leave much space for the Spirit to blow as he willed on each

---

5   See his book on the Spirit in the Pauline letters, *God's Empowering Presence* (Peabody, Mass: Hendrickson, 1994).
6   See *The Epistle to the Romans*, Black's New Testament Commentaries (London: A&C Black, 1957, 1991) p 18.

occasion. The *Didache* (a manual of Church order probably dating from the second century), for example, gives clear instruction about the structure of the eucharist and reveals some eucharistic textual material, but it also encourages the ministry of the word to be as long as seems right on the day and allows 'the prophets to give thanks as much as they wish.' And the *Odes of Solomon* (a rich, poetic text probably dating from the early second century) displays many of the themes of contemporary charismatic worship and clear allusions to the liturgical worship of the church, including its fundamentally trinitarian structure.[7]

The mix of form and freedom continued into the third century. I remember being in one of Geoffrey Cuming's lectures on the worship of the early church. Geoffrey, one of the great liturgical scholars of this century, was waxing eloquent on the eucharistic prayer of the *Apostolic Tradition of Hippolytus*, the earliest example of a complete eucharistic prayer in our possession. One member of the class who was not entirely friendly towards liturgy or its devotees rather rudely interrupted the flow with a question. 'Did leaders of worship really say all this stuff every time? Didn't they sometimes *busk it?*' Geoffrey chuckled and to most people's surprise said 'Yes that's a very good way of putting it. Some did "busk it." If they were good enough they made up their own prayers but *this* is the sort of thing they were expected to say in their prayers. Hippolytus' prayer is essentially an example of good practice.' What applied at the eucharist would have applied as much and probably more in other acts of worship. Standards of good liturgical practice had developed. Texts were evolving. Some, such as the Lord's Prayer and baptismal creed, were pretty much fixed. But there was still a lot of space for the Spirit to guide the worship and inspire worship leaders.

Avoiding Unnecessary Polarities

This all-too-quick glance at the formative period of Christian worship shows that the polarity which modern Christians perceive between fixed and free worship is not true to the actual working of the Spirit in worship. The *Prayer Book mentality* in which everything must be done by the book and the *liturgy free zone mentality* in which nothing must be in a book, have put asunder what God the Spirit has joined together. The unbiblical and, of course, unrealistic divide between free and fixed forms of worship has been institutionalized in English religion since the seventeenth century. Very crudely and briefly, three liturgical views came to expression in the seventeenth century and were set in the concrete of denominational divisions.

The Quaker view was that the light of the Spirit can be trusted to shine in each moment of worship. Everything which is not of the moment therefore is

---

7   For the text of the Odes see H F D Sparks (ed), *The Apocryphal Old Testament* (Oxford: OUP, 1984). I am grateful to my colleague Keith Hubbard for drawing my attention to the Odes.

dead. Liturgies (and even their accompanying sacraments) attempt to mediate past activities of the Spirit to the present. True worship relies on the immediate movement of the Spirit touching the heart of all true worshippers with the direct reality of God's presence and moving them to respond as God wills.

The Puritan view was that congregations should be given a good deal of freedom to respond to God in worship according to the particular work of the Spirit amongst them. But in order to support and safeguard this activity, worship leaders need advice about structuring worship, examples of good prayers and encouragement to ensure that congregations know a limited number of set texts. Puritanism therefore provided its ministers with the *Westminster Directory*, essentially a worship resource book.

The Anglican view was that to nurture and to sustain the fellowship and common life given by the Spirit, and to ensure that the truth into which we have been led by the Spirit is preserved, the structure and texts of worship must be prescribed and, if necessary, enforced. Anglicanism gave us the *Book of Common Prayer* to do the job.

All three views have their strengths but history has taught us that all three have serious weaknesses and need counter-balancing by other views. The exciting thing about liturgy in the Church of England at this stage of its life is that all three views are being held together in one encouragingly holistic and wholesome panorama. Carefully devised structures are given, often with suggested sub-structures within the main frame. Resources are provided in the form of mandatory texts (core texts, critical to our Christian formation), useful additional texts and a great variety of seasonal or thematic material. Space is allowed for the Spirit to weave the resources into the structures through the planning of worship and to inspire new things in the event of worship.

Spirit and Institution

The history of the church is full of times of great creativity, followed by a steady process of institutionalization. In the early church such institutional structures were necessary to enable ministries given by the Spirit to be more effective (see for example the selection of deacons in Acts 6). As the church has developed, so creative episodes have been typified more by their mould-breaking characteristics, where old structures have been torn apart to allow something new. But even here it does not take long for some kind of institution to grow up: in recent years it has been instructive to watch the 'House Churches' create structures which make them as denominational as the rest of us.[8]

A positive view of the interplay between charism and institution would be that where power is channelled it is enabled to work to great effect. More nega-

---

8 See G Coates (ed), *Breaking the Mould* (Eastbourne: Kingsway, 1993) for a good example of this.

tively it is easy to point to examples of institutionalization which have acted effectively to quench the Spirit. Those who work within structures of worship must always keep alert to the possibility that the structures can both enable and disable. Within the wider institution we need to act both as watchmen and stewards of the work of the Spirit in creation and renewal. The Church of England is in just such a period of upheaval and needs people who can work with the Spirit within the structures we have been given.[9]

The late 1990s are an opportune time for the Church of England. Our liturgies are being completely re-written, based upon the principle that structure is the basis of all we do, and offering as many alternative texts as doctrine and unity will allow. We view this from different perspectives. Chris is a member of the Liturgical Commission, which provides the initial texts from which Synod works. I am a member of General Synod, and more particularly a member of one of its Revision Committees. Even here, from within one of the most bureaucratic (and nit-picking) processes of any denomination in the land, it is possible to see the Creator Spirit at work, bringing together charism and institution.

The Liturgical Commission has an eye both on the needs of the present, and on the lessons (and great texts) of the past. Clearly it is possible to abuse the past work of the Spirit by giving new worshippers 'edited highlights' only, but the interplay of historic texts which have proved their worth, together with newly coined prayers and structures, is a real echoing of the householder who brings out 'treasures both new and old' (Matt 13.52).

The cynic might say that charismatics will need to exercise more faith than sight in believing that the Holy Spirit is at work in the Liturgical Commission of the Church of England! Perhaps it is easier to recognize the work of the creator Spirit in the creation of new prayers and innovations within worship. In the last twenty-five years the post-Communion prayer which begins 'Father of all...' in Rite A has found a key place in many people's spirituality, and was especially written for *Series 3*. Another example might be the prayers of preparation for ministry teams found in the early draft of the new Healing Services, which are a clear response to the proliferation of such teams in the renewal movement.

My experience is that the way the Church of England creates its liturgy, though time consuming and frustrating, is also honouring to the way the Spirit works with God's people. Texts and structures are offered, tried out by worshippers 'on the ground,' discussed, checked doctrinally, and tested to see if they are 'received' by those who will regularly use them. This process can be seen as opening up liturgical change not only to the *creator* Spirit, but also to the Spirit of *truth* and the Spirit of *fellowship*, by asking: 'Can these texts be used by all people everywhere?' The processes of Synod are also designed to enable the Spirit of

---

9   The recent completion of the 'Turnbull' process is just one sign of a renewal of structures undertaken by the General Synod.

unity: Revision Committees are deliberately made up of lay and ordained, male and female, with different flavours of church tradition. I have found that unity can and does break out!

The guiding principle of the creation of new liturgies in the Church of England, at least since *Lent, Holy Week, Easter,* is that basic structures and a core of mandatory texts should be fleshed out by a variety of resources, appropriately used in the local context. The provision of authorized texts guards against doctrinal aberrations while the offering of alternatives (or even the encouragement of local creativity) allows congregations to do what works, rather than what is imposed. Here, in the centre of what could be a dusty institution is the possibility of local initiative shaped in the family likeness of the wider church, based on a common core which is the gift of the Spirit to the universal church. The Spirit is concerned with relatedness, not cloning, and many would see the current wind of change in our liturgy as being driven by the authentic wind of the Spirit.

Spirit, Preparation and Delivery

Clearly the Spirit is at work not only through the history of the church and in our present-day structures, but also in the everyday life of congregations and in their regular acts of worship. No more eager intercession is made than by the worship leader or musician desperate to find some appropriate prayers or songs for the third Sunday in Lent! Yet it is often felt (perhaps at an unconscious level) that to prepare is to quench the Spirit, that the only true sermon is that where the notes are set aside, the only true worship time the one which emerged completely unplanned after a time of prayer.

I do not doubt that some sermons are inspired moment by moment, and that worship times *do* sometimes 'just happen,' but I believe that this is not the way the Spirit usually works. The church at Thessalonica was instructed not to 'quench' the Spirit, particularly in the realm of prophecy (1 Thess 5.19). The warning was to a church which might sideline the active participation of the Spirit in its worship, and the command could almost be expressed thus: 'Prepare to receive words of prophecy in all your services, and plan to have them tested.' It would seem that the Thessalonians were not yet 'put[ting] out the Spirit's fire' (NIV), and that their instruction was to put a good structure into place to enable the Spirit to work more effectively. Generations of worship leaders can testify to good preparation allowing freedom of the Spirit, and the use of gifts both 'decently and in order' (1 Cor 14.40).

Speaking about preaching, Martyn Lloyd Jones says: 'The Spirit generally uses a man's best preparation. It is not the Spirit or preparation; it is preparation plus the unction and the anointing and that which the Holy Spirit alone can supply.'[10] His ministry of preaching was founded on this 'double anointing' of

---

10 In *The Christian Soldier*, p 135, quoted in Tony Sargeant, *The Sacred Anointing* (London: Hodder and Stoughton, 1994) p 54.

preparation and delivery, and he would often wait in the pulpit for a sense of the Spirit resting on his words. In planning worship, the key act of preparation is ensuring that there is time for the Spirit to work within the service itself. Liturgy rightly gets a bad press when the service is so buttoned-up that God could not get a word in even if he wanted to. All worship leaders need to know the anointing of the Spirit on their leadership, so that good preparation will allow them to depart from the text, or deliver it in such a way that space can be made for appropriate response.

A recent book on spirituality is called *Patterns not Padlocks*.[11] Its title well sums up the work of the Spirit in worship as ideally practised week by week in churches across the land. Liturgy is there to give pattern and shape, allowing depth and breadth, as well as a surprise or two. Too often a bad experience of being padlocked has put charismatics off, and an equally bad experience of having no pattern at all has quenched the Spirit's work for those hesitantly dabbling a spiritual toe in the living waters. The following two chapters look at positive views of liturgy, and then at how a service which is avowedly formal can itself be open to the dynamic and active work of the Spirit.

3

Liturgy and the Work of the People

There is No Act of Worship Which is Not Liturgical

This statement is only true if its terms are defined! If 'liturgy' only meant set texts which admitted of no deviation, it would plainly be false. But if liturgy is seen as core texts with a basic structure which allows different acts of worship to unfold, then it begins to make more sense. A defining moment in my own experience came at a major house church conference in the early 1980s. We sang 'Majesty' eighteen times without a break, and many gifts of the Spirit were manifested. It suddenly struck me that, however freely we had worshipped, however much the Spirit was given a free role, and however much the platform was defining itself in opposition to churches hide-bound in tradition, the main speaker always began his address at the same time each night. Since then I have always looked for the hidden structure which defines 'free' worship, not to expose it as secretly 'liturgical,' but simply to see how each worshipping community settles into an order with which it is comfortable.

---

11 Angela Ashwin, *Patterns not Padlocks* (Eagle, 1994).

Every act of worship has some structure. Common sense suggests that someone has decided what time the meeting will start, who will lead, what music there will be, and who will speak. Even a community which has decided to make a worship time completely open has actually *decided* to do this, and gradually habits form as to who will do what. Congregations which worship regularly together get into a rhythm, and develop a style, not only because a desire for some kind of order is part of our humanity, but also because the Spirit gifts people to offer complementary ministries which the same people tend to express (some are prophets, others teachers, etc).[12] In this sense the liturgy is about the *enacted expectations* of the gathering: 'what have we gathered for, and who will put it into practice?'

A more technical question might be this: what needs to happen in this act of worship for it to be truly *performative* for us? Perfomative language is that which actually *does* something when uttered ('I take you to be my husband'; 'I name this ship,' and so on).[13] For such language to *work* the right words must be used in the right place at the right time by the right people. It is easy to extend this to a complete act of worship. Whether an act of worship is *seen as* worship by the worshippers will depend on whether their *self-understanding* is matched by the *ritual* in which they take part. Have the right things taken place, and the right words been said and sung? The way these questions are answered helps define what makes worship worship, or what the liturgy is for that particular gathering.[14]

Some congregations or denominations would point to a defined set of texts in order to answer the question. Others would speak more generally about anointed leaders, words tested by the gathering, or good songs being sung in a suitable order. In its widest sense, all of this is liturgy.

Liturgy Expressing the Here and Now

A key feature of liturgical change this century has been the provision of seasonal and other resources. Alternative confessions and creeds enable particular themes to be explored even at fixed points in the service. Flexible structures, together with a variety of written texts, now enable congregations to use appropriate words at different points in their worshipping lives. Those of us raised in this period of liturgical ferment find it hard to imagine what life was like using the same words week in, week out. Although even then there were different weekly readings and collects, together with variable psalms and hymns, it re-

---

12 I take 1 Cor 14.26 ('when you come together, each one has a hymn...etc') to be a description of certain people regularly offering these gifts, as well as of direct inspiration of individuals on a one-off basis.

13 There is a growing body of writing on performative language. The standard work is J L Austin, *How to Do Things with Words* (Oxford: OUP, 1962).

14 An interesting application of this to the anointing of the sick can be found in Joseph J Schaller, 'Performative Language Theory: An Exercise in the Analysis of Ritual' *Worship* 62 (1988).

mains the case that today's worshippers have a far greater opportunity to create contextually appropriate liturgies than our predecessors ever did.

This illustrates one of the gifts of structured and planned worship. With thought it enables a gathering fully to express itself in worship to God. The paradox of worship is that as we offer ourselves fully to God, so God offers himself fully to us. Our offering is only in response to what God has already done for us, and can only be offered in and through Christ, in the power of the gift of the Spirit. In that sense liturgy has a two-fold task—to enable us to offer *what* we are, *where* we are, and to express to us all that God is and always has been, both *here* and *everywhere*.

The point of this is simply to say that though new liturgies inevitably express changes in world-view and new concerns (a greater emphasis on creation and issues about gender are two areas which come to mind), the purpose of liturgy is to allow local congregations to make *their* offering as the focal point of the universal church. Worship in the centre of a major city, with a background of sirens and traffic, feels very different from worship in a tiny village, with the noise of tractors and cows underpinning the psalms. We worship from where we are, and the provision of *A Service of the Word* in 1994 came as a direct response to the need of congregations in Urban Priority Areas to find a worshipping voice which is truly authentic.[15]

In 1 Corinthians 12 Paul outlines the Spirit's work in giving different gifts, while remaining the Spirit of unity. There need be no problem with different congregations offering differing acts of worship, and expressing the different gifts they have been given, as long as the basis of faith and a denominational 'family likeness' remain. A good liturgy will give worshippers resources, texts and structures to express what they have been given by God: a rural or urban setting; people from different generations; the glory of a magnificent building; or a servant heart for a needy community. In the same way different services might express particular points in the congregation's life: a farewell; a new start; pastoral rites; a giving campaign, and so on. Liturgy offers the congregation the chance to express what God is doing *here and now*, both in the words used, and in the participation of many members within it.

Liturgy Expressing the Always and Everywhere

In his creative and demanding study of the Spirit's work, Michael Welker describes how the Spirit 'connects intense experiences of individuality with a new experience of community.'[16] This certainly rings true to the experience of charismatics in general and to charismatic worship in particular. The deeply individual and intimate work of the Spirit renews love in us for our brothers

---

15 *A Service of the Word* (London: CHP, 1994).
16 Michael Welker, *God the Spirit* (Minneapolis: Fortress Press, 1994) p 233.

and sisters in Christ and creates a desire to be with those whom the Spirit has similarly touched. The Spirit's work is truly personal because it meets us in the depths of our basic human need for relationship. Although the Spirit may take us to the solitude of the mountain to be with God (Luke 6.12; 9.28), he sends us back again into the community of shared living (Luke 6.13; 9.37).

Charismatic worship can look at times like a highly individualistic affair. People appear so intent on their own engagement with God that they seem to disengage with those around them. No doubt in its worst forms this does happen. But even then charismatic worshippers know that they cannot do it alone. They rely on a group of people together to be similarly engaged. Even in the privatized appearance of some forms of charismatic worship there is an underlying recognition that worship is a communal experience. In its better and best forms, charismatic worship involves a demonstrated experience of mutuality between worshippers (see 1 Cor 12.10b). The various members of the body in their various ministries all contribute, by the one Spirit, to the edification of the people and to the praise of God (1 Cor 12–14).

Just as the Spirit moves our hearts to sing one song together in worship— even at times one song with different tongues—so the Spirit also gives us words which connect us with a much wider Christian community. The prayer known as the 'Grace' is a good example. This text, which affirms the fellowship of the Holy Spirit, allows Christians of different backgrounds, traditions and nationalities to share in a simple trinitarian greeting and blessing. By their very nature worship songs tend not to last long.[17] Despite their ability to spread rapidly across continents they are inevitably limited to particular times, cultures, age-groups and spiritualities. The Grace provides a fixed point transcending all these fast-changing features of human life.

As well as offering a fixed point of connection with Christians throughout the world, the Grace also connects us with the church throughout its history. It takes us back to the Corinthian church and quite probably to other New Testament communities from whom Paul may well have inherited the formula. I find it moving to have fellowship with the New Testament church in this short set of words. I find it moving to have fellowship with the disciples and with Jesus of Nazareth as I say the Lord's Prayer. I find it moving to have fellowship with the fourth-century church with its determined insistence to express the full divinity of Christ and the Spirit, when I join with the church of today in proclaiming the Nicene-Constantinople Creed. Liturgy gives us a concrete connection with the universal church both in its present (geographical) breadth and in its past (historical) depth.

---

17 See John Leach, *Hymns and Spiritual Songs* (Grove Worship Series No 132).

Common Worship

To worship *in common* with others has been one of the fundamental values of Anglican worship. The *Book of Common Prayer* was an attempt to unite the worshipping nation in a shared experience of worship. In the sixteenth century it aimed to overcome the diversification of the various local medieval rites and to give people the liturgy in the language of common life. In the seventeenth century it aimed to overcome the fragmentation endemic to Protestantism. We may have reservations over how it sought to achieve this ideal but we cannot dismiss its underlying concern for an audibly shared experience of worship.

Despite our very different cultural and ecclesiastical culture, there remains a deep instinct in the Church of England to maintain some form of common identity in its varied worship. For some time the Liturgical Commission has spoken of the spectrum of congregations being bound together by common core texts and structures.[18] The compilers of *Celebrating Common Prayer* sought to offer a form of daily prayer which a wide variety of people and groups could share. The General Synod has welcomed the proposal that the new generation of liturgy should be called *Common Worship*. All this is a sign of the Spirit of fellowship at work holding members of the body of Christ together in a joint expression of worship.

Common words of worship are intended to express a common faith in God. That is the merit of shared texts. They have been through the sieve of truth. Every attempt has been made to tease heresy out of them. Liturgy therefore helps to preserve and proclaim the universal faith of the Church. It ensures that we are truly *orthodox*—that we offer right worship, worship that is theologically sound.

One of the weaknesses of the Quaker and Puritan liturgical positions mentioned earlier, was that when the doctrine of the Trinity went out of theological fashion in the eighteenth century, much of the Quaker and Puritan (both congregational and presbyterian) traditions slipped all too easily into unitarianism—a place from which Quaker worship today finds itself difficult to escape. The same theological forces were pressing against the Church of England and many of its theologians and parochial clergy went in a similar direction. But Anglicanism's commitment to a trinitarian liturgy enabled it to be more successful in preserving the trinitarian faith in its public face and, thereby, in the devotions of its worshippers than the other traditions.[19]

There is always a danger that the charismatic movement and particularly its worship will repeat the mistakes of history. Liturgy can help to safeguard against

---

18 See Michael Perham (ed), *The Renewal of Common Prayer* (London: CHP/SPCK, 1993).
19 I have recently taken part in a number of communion services in the 'non-textual' end of the URC. On each occasion I have been intrigued to find that, despite the emphasis on the Spirit in seventeenth century Puritanism, the Spirit hardly received a mention in these late twentieth century celebrations.

this tendency. An interesting example of the imposition of liturgy for this very purpose happened at St Andrew's, Chorleywood. Some time ago one member of the clergy team used to extemporize the eucharistic prayer when he presided. I was always impressed by the structure and content of these prayers, even if a little surprised by their unguardedly strong sacramental language. David Pytches, who was vicar at the time, had a similar reaction but, as the person responsible for the building up of the people, he decided that the complexity and subtlety of sacramental doctrine required the use of a prayer that had been through the careful controls of authorization. In this heartland of charismatic worship the risk of extemporized prayer upsetting a delicate doctrinal balance was felt to be too great.

The Spirit of *truth* and *fellowship* has been and continues to be active in the formation of liturgical texts that hold safely Christian doctrine and relate closely Christian believers. This life-sustaining work of the Spirit is to be discerned and received.

4

The Spirit and Liturgy in Practice

Routine Worship and the Spirit

Many people have experienced the sinking feeling towards the end of some large Christian gathering when they realize that they have to go home to the ordinary routine. One vicar welcomed back a group of Spring Harvesters with the words 'Don't worry, it'll wear off soon enough.' This booklet came out of just that experience. At the end of New Wine one year it suddenly hit me that I was going back to lead Rite A! It was not enough to comfort myself with the knowledge that New Wine or Spring Harvest have their own liturgies; the difference between *celebration* worship, where openness is the key, and *congregational* worship, where order and regularity are prized, is great. How then can our regular diet be open to the Spirit in the way that we expect one-off events to be?

The first thing to realize is that celebration and congregational worship function in different ways. Knowing that you are to return to worship next week, and the week after that, changes the dynamic, and requires an acceptance of structure and order. There is a blessing in the 'common round'—the regular use of central texts, and the familiarity with a rhythm of worship allow for the deep work of the Spirit in the routine of our daily lives. Many conferences rely on a limited repertoire of songs and hymns, whereas routine worship needs to have a broader diet. Variety brings nourishment, as long as worship leaders can keep track of the frequency with which certain items are used.

Similarly, conference worship may concentrate on limited Bible readings. Routine worship requires some kind of pattern of Bible reading. Congregations quickly tire of being at the whim of their leaders, and preachers often like to have some idea of what they are to speak on in the coming weeks. Bible reading in the Church of England is governed by the Lectionary, and it has been instructive to spend three years in a church which (illegally, though not unusually) designed its own, followed by three years in one which adheres strictly to the *ASB*. Any lectionary challenges you with texts you would not normally choose. Luther called the Bible his 'adversary,' and the Spirit is able to impress lessons upon us which we might not expect, even as we wrestle with passages that no one would ever underline by choice.

The new three-year Lectionary can only aid this process.[20] In the 'green' season the Bible is freed to speak without being fettered by themes. In special seasons the wider choice of readings allows more Scripture to be read, and there is now permission to depart from set readings at certain times. No lectionary will ever be perfect, and the Spirit may well make it clear that your congregation needs Amos *now*. My experience is that set readings are no more nor less 'spiritual' than any other method, and that a carefully crafted lectionary has the ability to be used by the Spirit to give people a wide exposure to the word of God. Time and again it seems that the readings are just right this week!

Related to this, the Christian year is a great resource for teaching and experiencing the breadth and depth of Christian discipleship. I once served in a church which did not 'do' Lent one year (because another topic was deemed to be more important), and it soon became clear that we had missed the opportunity to consider the need for penitence and obedience as a way of preparing for the passion, death and resurrection of Christ. In the Christian year we are offered themes of preparation, expectation, revelation, incarnation, penitence, discipleship, and resurrection hope. Careful and sensitive observance of the gift we are given here can be a fruitful ground for the Spirit's work of conviction of sin, convincing in the truth, bringing of new life, and leading into hope. Some traditions make great play of the renewal of baptismal vows at certain points in the year, particularly at Easter. Why not remind people of the cleansing and renewing work of the Spirit, if such a service is offered to us?[21]

---

20 For a clear introduction see T Lloyd, P Moger, J Sinclair, M Vasey, *Introducing the New Lectionary* (Grove Worship Series No 141). Mark Earey has produced an invaluable aid for introducing the new lectionary, The PRAXIS Lectionary Training Pack, available from Institute for Liturgy and Mission, Sarum College, 19 The Close, Salisbury, SP1 2EE.
21 See Alan Wilkinson and Christopher Cocksworth (eds), *An Anglican Companion* (London: SPCK, 1996) pp 122-123, for a clear and helpful guide to the church year.

Making Room for the Spirit

The chief charismatic argument against formal services is that they leave no room for the Spirit. Formal worshippers would counter that it is frightening and disabling not to know what is going to happen next. After a simple said eucharist in an otherwise overtly charismatic church one worshipper said to me that 'it was so good not to be taken by surprise'! It is possible to be both open and ordered. All services require some structure. Even in those where the structure and texts are to the fore, room can (and should) still be made.

I have found that the spontaneity of the Spirit is actually enabled by planning and structure. Where it is felt to be important to 'listen' to the Spirit, it is possible to do this *before* the service, and offer the resulting words, visions, prophecies and pictures at a set point in the service itself. This can easily be followed by a time of silence, together with an opportunity for ministry either at that point or later. Many churches have 'listening teams' which operate in this way, and praying beforehand can be a useful way of gathering all the participants in a service to focus on the task ahead. It can also be deeply affirming for the recipients of such 'words' that God was already at work while they were on their way to worship. One of the most powerful times I can remember was when a children's group had such a listening time, and had their words read out when they re-entered the main service. This was followed by a time of ministry as people in the congregation responded. However it happens, the liturgy for this can be quite formal and non-threatening, and in one church this fitted easily into a Rite B sung Communion service.

A key feature of renewal is the opportunity for prayer ministry to be offered. Again, formal services do not preclude this: many churches offer it during the administration of communion, either at the rail or in another part of the building. At Skegby such ministry is now commonplace and widely used, where I believe few would respond to an open call to 'come out' for ministry in a less formal setting. A simple instruction is given, usually at the invitation to receive communion, but occasionally after the sermon, or during the notices. Wise advice makes this ministry both public and semi-formal, so as to guard against it becoming counselling, for which another context is necessary. Its public nature asserts that prayer ministry is part of the whole ministry of the church, not a hole-in-the-corner affair. It is easy to set up structures to allow follow-up ministry to take place if necessary.

If we believe that God speaks today through the word as Christians worship, it is logical that people should be given the opportunity to respond. The order of service printed on our notice sheet in Nottingham always contained the word 'response' after the sermon, and such response was a formal part of the liturgy there. It was the duty of the service leader to lead this time, which might include tongues, interpretation, words and prophecies. Occasionally all that was needed was silence, sometimes the music group were primed with a song, and once the only logical response was for us all to leave the building and pray in the market place. Sadly we chickened out of this, but the word would not go away, and soon a group went out to pray each week, to the great benefit of the church's ministry.

John Leach in his Grove booklet, *Responding to Preaching* talks of the lack of expectation as regards immediate response to the Word of God.[22] Building it in as a formal part of the service can begin to address this for many people. We are just beginning to do this at Skegby, mainly by having a time of quiet, followed by an appropriate song, and a suggested action (for example the opportunity to receive ministry later). It is important to phrase your instructions carefully though: I once told a congregation after a powerful sermon by a national figure that *now* it was time to listen to *God*. She rightly asked what we had been doing up until that point.

Similarly, it is possible to build in a time for the use of spiritual gifts. In the second century the *Didache* highlighted the importance of giving the prophets space to prophesy. Though it may be that Paul's instructions to the Corinthians were about restricting and ordering such prophesy, his command to do *'all things decently and in order'* can be heard to be as much about doing *'all* things' as about being decent. Clearly this raises issues of manipulation, but it is possible to say that after the next song or hymn there will be a time where gifts may be exercised as an *encouragement* rather than a command. John Leach has given us the term 'planned spontaneous happenings,' which I now find a helpful part of liturgy.[23] Here we simply plan to be open, and as long as the worshippers know who is presiding at this point, then all can be encouraged to step out a little in faith. It is vital to know who is steering the ship here, and to know that the ship will be moved on at some point sooner or later. If you are in safe hands you are enabled to experiment a little more.[24]

Others have written about the use of *music* in worship.[25] I have found that replacing one hymn with two or three songs strung together completely transforms an act of worship, without being too 'way out,' given that music would normally be happening then anyway. We often put this spot just before the gospel, or after the sermon, and combined with silence or a well-led response time, this music performs a function which a hymn is simply not designed to do. Sung worship before the service and during the administration of communion can also be very effective, especially if people are encouraged to worship with it,

22 John Leach. *Responding to Preaching* (Grove Worship Series No 139) p 5.
23 John Leach. *Liturgy and Liberty* (Eastbourne: MARC, 1989) p 155.
24 This concept of 'steering' (taken from an interpretation of 'kubernesis,' the gift of administration in 1 Cor 12.28), together with that of presidency, is well handled in Colin Buchanan's, *Leading Worship* (Grove Worship Series No 76) pp 1-9.
25 See particularly John Leach, *Hymns and Spiritual Songs*, and Peter Moger, *Music and Worship: Principles to Practice* (Grove Worship Series No 127).

and not simply have it as a pleasant background over which to talk.

More practically, one of the advantages of formal worship is that people generally have a clear idea of the *timing* of the service. This becomes crucial when children's groups are returning, or when clergy have to get to another service that morning. I often reflect, irreverently, that the Holy Spirit always seems to require fifteen minutes more than is available, even at celebration meetings, but my experience is that a timetable does not of itself restrict the working of the Spirit. Things just happen *differently*, and where ministry might have a slot to itself in a less pressured service, in a busy morning service it happens while other elements continue. It does not honour God if the adults are having a tremendous time inside while the children are neglected elsewhere.

A Framework for Openness

Technically, up until the mid 1990s, the Church of England only provided liturgies which had to be prized apart in order to be open and flexible. Careful reading of Rite A does reveal plenty of rubrics such as 'in these or other suitable words,' and alternative structures are offered, but by and large it is more difficult to come off the tram lines than to stay on them. *A Service of the Word* has changed that completely. What is authorized here, as a main service of Morning or Evening Prayer, is a structure only. Texts, hymns and liturgical happenings are to be inserted as appropriate, with the assumption that a planning team will put such services together.

Though *A Service of the Word* and its associated resource volume, *Patterns for Worship*[26] were conceived as a response to the need for appropriate worship in UPAs, and as a way of giving necessary shape to often formless Family Services, it seems to me that they also give us a superb framework for being open to the Spirit. Readings from an authorized lectionary are assumed, along with a range of worship resources (including scriptural songs and psalms). Instructions are given about the inclusion of a collect, intercessions and the Lord's Prayer, and an authorized Affirmation of Faith, together with an authorized confession and absolution. Beyond that, the service is open, and no other texts are imposed. Churches are therefore given the Anglican essentials in a way that will allow them to express their own life, offer their own gifts, be open to the work of the Spirit, and still be part of the church catholic. Here is liturgy at its best, resourcing and giving shape to the work of the Spirit for a church's regular worship.

Liturgies for Renewal

Many churches are now setting aside particular services for 'celebration' or 'renewal' events, either as part of the regular diet of worship, or as set-piece midweek or weekend happenings. The question then arises as to what form

---

26 (London: CHP, 1995).

these should take.

If such services are not the main act of worship for the parish, Church of England rules cease to apply, and even the constraints imposed by *A Service of the Word* can be set aside. It is worth giving careful thought as to what to discard though, in that it may still be appropriate to have an affirmation of faith, or time of confession. Corporate intercession, perhaps using a variety of models, may also work well. I have been in renewal events where we have prayed silently, prayed in groups, prayed out loud one by one, prayed out loud all together (which takes some courage but is good on participation), prayed in tongues, walked around and within a building, and used visual images and incense (for the prayers of the saints, Rev 8.4)—though not all at the same time!

Thought also needs to be given as to how the Bible will be read, how music will be used, and how all will be fitted into a structure. If the event is to be a healing service, new liturgies are being produced (as part of the Initiation package) which contain numerous resources (including laments, a neglected part of healing services in many renewal contexts). For celebration events a classic pattern is (sung) worship, teaching and ministry, though it need not always be this way, and some events have begun ministry immediately after worship, with teaching following on.

In all this it helps to find a flexible framework. A classic Vineyard pattern, described by Barry Liesch has served many events well.[27] It starts with a call to worship, or *invitation*, continues with encouragement in worship, or *engagement*, moves into *exaltation* (focussing on God's transcendence), then *adoration* (God's immanence), leading to *intimacy*, where worshippers can fully express their worship of Abba, Father. At the end of this it is necessary to 'close out,' so that the service can move on, ministry can start, or the service can end! As a pattern it can shape the choice of songs at the beginning, or indeed a whole event, and it is possible to concentrate on certain aspects more than others. A good response to preaching might be a time of adoration leading into intimacy, for example.

In any renewal event the initial question is a liturgical one: what will the shape be, and what resources shall we use? Another question is more practical, but also relates to good liturgical practice: who will preside? Often there will be multiple leaders (as in many diocesan events). In this case it is vital for the congregation's sake that leadership is clearly handed on, and that leaders should be both named and visible. A third question is about participation. Is it enough for the congregation to sing a lot, or are there other things they can do? Versicles and responses may seem a little churchy, but they gather people together, and many a celebration has proclaimed 'The Lord is here, His Spirit is with us,' to surprising effect.

---

27 B Liesch, *People in the Presence of God* (Crowborough: Highland, 1988) pp 91-94.

5
Conclusion

At an early stage of planning this booklet we had to ask ourselves the question as to whether you could be both a charismatic and a liturgist. We have been expected to apologise for being both, depending on where we were at the time! Many said we were 'brave' to do the New Wine seminar from which this booklet evolved. Charismatics have clearly taken worship to themselves, but is not liturgy something like trainspotting—a hobby which is fun for some, but has little to do with where God is really at work?

At the end of this process we believe even more strongly that charismatics need liturgy at its best, and that liturgy needs charismatics at their best. The renewal of the entire liturgy of the Church of England is a huge opportunity for worship to be placed at the centre of every congregation in the land. Liturgy has a power to 'sum up' an act of worship, to offer the essentials and the breadth of our faith, and to connect the church militant with the church triumphant and the church universal. It also has the capacity to be stultifyingly boring, and to miss the point that Christians gather to offer worship, not just to engage in a ritual. A charismatic expectation that God might actually do something this morning which will take us by surprise is an essential ingredient of any act of worship which seeks to join with the company of heaven.

In all this the experience of the assembly in 2 Chronicles is instructive. An elaborate liturgy had been devised and rehearsed to celebrate the building of the Temple. When God arrived and filled the place with a cloud, all that had been planned ground to a halt because 'the priests could not stand to minister' (2 Chron 5.13–14). May we so plan, pray and worship that God fills our services and celebrations with his tangible presence, to his praise and glory.